THE SECRET LIFE OF THE
KRAKEN

by Benjamin Harper

CAPSTONE PRESS
a capstone imprint

Published by Capstone Press, an imprint of Capstone
1710 Roe Crest Drive, North Mankato, Minnesota 56003
capstonepub.com

Library of Congress Cataloging-in-Publication Data is available on the Library
of Congress website.

ISBN: 9781669004110 (hardcover)
ISBN: 9781669040439 (paperback)
ISBN: 9781669004073 (ebook PDF)

Summary: Readers take a look into the secret life of the kraken to uncover
surprising facts, including where it lives, how it catches fish, and more.

Editorial Credits
Editor: Abby Huff; Designer: Heidi Thompson; Media Researcher: Jo Miller;
Production Specialist: Tori Abraham

Image Credits
Alamy: Album, 29, Chronicle, 19, Chronicle, 27 (giant squid), steeve-x-art, 21;
Avalon: Paulo de Oliveira, 24; Bridgeman Images: © Look and Learn, 11; Getty
Images: Claudia Prommegger, 13, John M Lund Photography Inc, 9; Science
Source, 16, 23, The Natural History Museum, London, 27 (suckers), Christion
Darkin, 5; Shutterstock: Aceng Zaenal Arifin, 7, Albina Poliakova, Cover (fishing
rod), Elegant Solution, 15 (Kraken), graficriver_icons_logo, 28 (glasses, hat,
mustache), LouieLea, 14, Paul Fleet, 25, Peter Hermes Furian, 15 (map),
shaineast, Cover (Kraken), StrongBrand, 28 (Kraken), Triff, 10, Vertes Edmond
Mihai, 12, Wikimedia: Anonymous, 17, T. G. B. Lloyd (1829–1876), 20

Design Elements
Shutterstock: Kues, Net Vector, Victoria Sergeeva

All internet sites appearing in back matter were available and accurate when
this book was sent to press.

Printed and bound in China. PO5132

TABLE OF CONTENTS

Words in **bold** are in the glossary.

MEET THE KRAKEN

Ahoy, matey! If you're a **sailor,** you've likely heard of the kraken. People have been talking about this sea monster for hundreds of years. But it might not be just the stuff of **legends**. Could the beast exist? Time to find out!

TAKE A CRACK AT THE KRAKEN

Are you a sea beast smartie? Test your kraken knowledge! Can you guess:

1. Its home?

2. Its reported body length?

3. What legends say it looks like?

4. What's said to be created when it dives down?

5. True or false? The secret of the kraken may be solved.

ANSWERS

1. The waters near Norway

2. 50 to 60 feet

3. A squid or octopus

4. Large **whirlpools**

5. True

LEGENDS OF THE BEAST

The kraken splashed onto the scene long ago. In 1180, the King of Norway first wrote about it. **Norse** sailors were likely telling tales before then.

Legends say the beast is big. It can be mistaken for an island! The kraken has many long arms. It has two giant eyes.

SEA ATTACK!

The kraken doesn't like visitors in its home. Old stories say it can sink ships! The kraken's arms rise up from the sea. They wrap on tight. They pull. Then down goes the ship. Sailors from hundreds of years ago were always on the lookout.

FACT
The sea beast's name comes from the Old Norse word *kraki*. It means boat hook or anchor.

GONE FISHING

Arms aren't the only thing the kraken uses to grab food. It uses poop as fish **bait**! That's what a report from the 1750s says. Kraken poo smells tasty to fish. They swim over. Then the kraken strikes! It gobbles its fishy meal.

HOME WATERS

The kraken keeps it cool. Legends say it lives in the chilly waters near Norway. It swims by Iceland and Greenland too.

Old maps often had drawings of the beast. Only the bravest sailors took to the seas. They knew they might run into a grumpy kraken.

North Pole

Arctic
Ocean

Greenland

Iceland

Norway

Atlantic
Ocean

KRAKEN CREW

The kraken has friends around Iceland. The hafgufa is a huge, fishy **cryptid**. It eats whales, ships, and anything it can catch.

The lyngbakr likes to pretend to be an island. Stories say sailors would land on the big beast's back. Then the sea monster would dive underwater. Rude!

CATCHING UP WITH THE KRAKEN

Who's the kraken, really? In 1857, scientist Japetus Steenstrup wanted to know. He studied sea life. He decided that kraken reports were describing a kind of squid. He gave the animal a scientific name. It's called the giant squid.

The kraken's life? Maybe not so secret anymore!

FACT

Steenstrup hadn't seen a giant squid. But he found a large squid beak that led him to think it existed.

POKE! POKE! WHO'S THERE?

In 1873, a Canadian fisherman saw a large object in the water. He poked it. A long arm shot up and grabbed his boat! The man shooed it off with an axe. The creature swam away in a squirt of ink. Did the man meet a giant squid, aka the kraken?

FACT

The fisherman had proof of his fight. He chopped off a 19-foot-long squid **tentacle**!

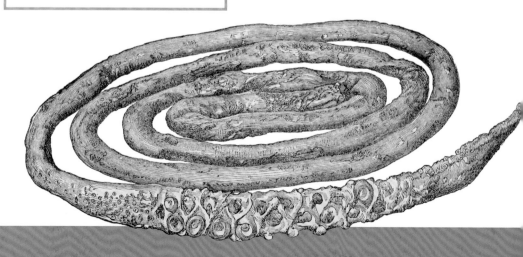

STINKY SQUID SHOW

Weeks later, other Canadian fishermen had a lucky catch. They netted a whole giant squid! A man named Moses Harvey bought it. He hung it in his bathtub and charged others to see it. The squid was 24 feet long. It had a serious stink!

FACT

Harvey's giant squid made history. It was the first whole one to be photographed.

SQUID SECRETS

Are giant squids behind the kraken legends? No one can be totally sure. But many scientists say it's a match.

Giant squids are hard to study. They live deep in the ocean. Scientists finally saw one in the wild for the first time in 2012!

a dead giant squid from 2016

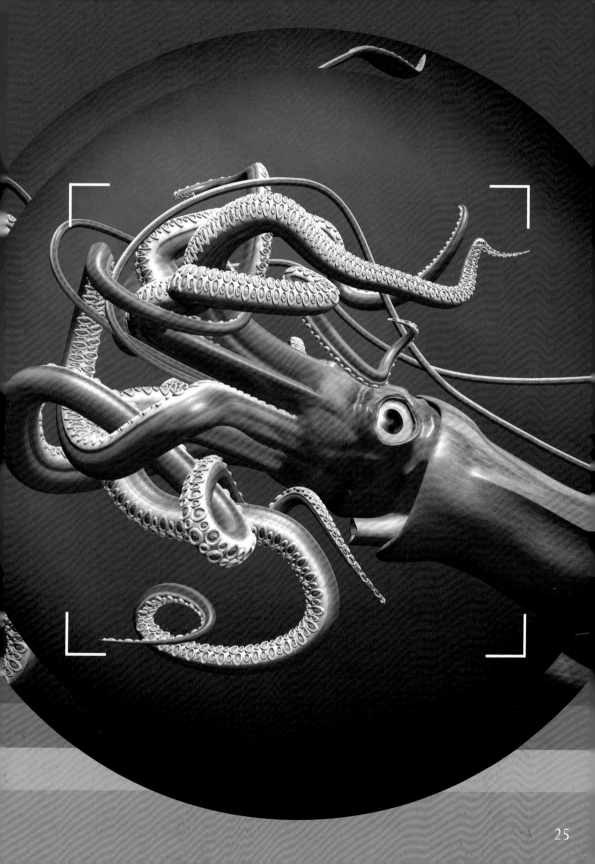

GIANT SQUID FACTS

What do scientists know about giant squids? The animal:

- Lives in the Midnight Zone. No sunlight reaches these deep ocean waters.

- Bites with a sharp birdlike beak.

- Grabs with eight arms and two tentacles. Each has suckers lined with teeth.

- Shoots ink to get away from danger.

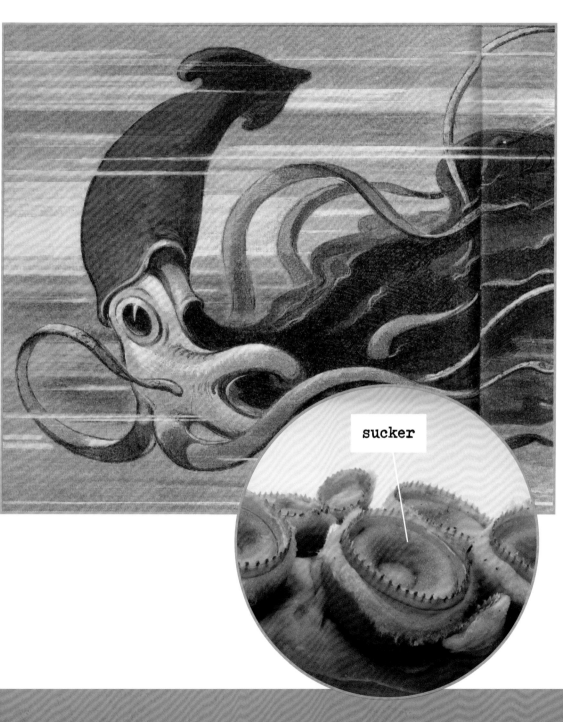

sucker

BIG SCREEN SPLASH

The kraken is a movie star. The beast attacks in *Pirates of the Caribbean: Dead Man's Chest*. It's also in *Clash of the Titans*. A famous line? "Release the kraken!"

The kraken appears on screens. But watch out at the beach. The real thing may show up!

GLOSSARY

bait (BEYT)—food used as a trap to catch animals

cryptid (KRYP-tid)—an animal that has not been proven to be real by science

legend (LEJ-uhnd)—a story passed down through the years that may or may not be entirely true

Norse (NORS)—having to do with ancient Scandinavia, which includes the modern-day countries Norway and Sweden

sailor (SAY-ler)—a person who works on a ship or boat

tentacle (TEN-tuh-kuhl)—on a squid, a long body part with suckers on the end that is used for grabbing food

whirlpool (WURL-pool)—water that moves quickly in a circle, which pulls in nearby objects

READ MORE

Andrews, Elizabeth. *Kraken: Gigantic Ocean Terror.* Minneapolis: Pop!, a division of ABDO, 2022.

Clarke, Ginjer L. *Are Sea Monsters Real?* New York: Penguin Young Readers, 2022.

Goddu, Krystyna Poray. *Sea Monsters: From Kraken to Nessie.* Minneapolis: Lerner Publications, 2017.

INTERNET SITES

Beano: 15 Mysterious Giant Squid Fun Facts
beano.com/posts/giant-squid-facts

PBS: Release the Kraken!
pbs.org/video/release-the-kraken-dzf76y/

Wonderopolis: What Was the Kraken?
wonderopolis.org/wonder/what-was-the-kraken

INDEX

ABOUT THE AUTHOR

Benjamin Harper lives in Los Angeles where he edits superhero books for a living. When he's not at work, he writes; watches monster movies; and hangs out with cats Marjorie and Jerry, a betta fish named Toby, and tanks full of rough-skinned and eastern newts.